ISBN 978-1-946433-89-3
First Edition, First Printing, 2022

Ugly Duckling Presse
The Old American Can Factory
232 Third Street #E-303
Brooklyn, NY 11215
uglyducklingpresse.org

Distributed in the USA by SPD/Small Press Distribution
Distributed in the UK by Inpress Books

Cover artwork by Walker Teiser
Photography by Jules Allen
Design and typesetting by dourmoose
The type is Garamond


Printed and bound at McNaughton & Gunn
Covers printed letterpress at Ugly Duckling Presse and offset at Prestige Printing

The publication of this book was made possible, in part, by a grant from the National Endowment for the Arts, by public funds from the New York City Department of Cultural Affairs in partnership with the City Council, and by the support of the New York State Council on the Arts with the support of the Office of the Governor and the New York State Legislature.
This project is supported by the Robert Rauschenberg Foundation.

Palm-Lined with Potience

Poems by
Basie Allen

Ugly Duckling Presse, 2022

*for my parents*
*Machelle and Jules*


*the most O'est*
*OGs*

*these poems*
*are to be read in the imaginary state*
*of a crowded Monday morning*
*somewhere between the idea*
*of Rocawear and Baudelaire*

# Pretty Is (2.0)

*Another Quatrain for Ma Dukes*


in the vanguard of my owned
blackness    O     I am the air
off the many so year-ago trees
that be the prettiest is of all


having been so here before
the dear darkness[1]
dear darkness:    needed weight
to wind and the goosebump too


I lay beneath your time
where exhaled breath
does not bereave its body
when it moves


for it knows to continue
into wind and all
without needing to ask
light for permissions


---

1   "...dear darkness" is not in direct reference to Kevin Young. Tho @ Kevin Young...
   what up! we should build – na' mean ?

# Haiku for Richard Wright

a negro's clothesline
of mostly clean undershirts
twists in evening winds

# An Answer for Jimmy Symington

*you asked me once what ◯ means*

                   so
tired as the tossed stone
plucked and flung off the rip
of the young shore's hand
— I sink

into puddled imprints
of wild paws

free ripples wash
over the seabed of my disco
ball black skin all fractal
once rivered
glisten

   (pause)

Motherwell
under seagull yaw

it is here
where I have learned
to write on both sides
of silence— the glitter
pained gauze

only holding my breath
to better hear the earth
when she sings to me

sweet boy  ◯  breathe

# In Dirt's Words

*Ars Poetica*

I let the black sun rise
before the reptile's first step
into fur-blooded hunger
could growl

before blue grew lips—
learned to crawl
into cradled arms of dawn

I let the black sun rise pre-wonder
    Aimé
as I whispered into mud years
baby    I love you

before juice of new eyes
    Césaire
could build up and spill

over naive cheeks
cushioned on both sides
of a hammocked smile

I let the black sun rise
before the weight of leaf rings
could rivet loose ends of centuries together

five billion wide open mouths
unhinge from hook bones

saying sweet things in the splinter
like baby I love you too

I let the black sun
    Romare
    rise

so the riff of the drum rock
Bearden
      could rattle over
      and over

before echos needed impulse
        mirrors needed ego

I let the black sun rise

       so   the   wild
     could   reach

over the other
side of horizons

unzip tamed eyes
from light needy feelings

fragrant and curly bodies
rusting in peace
under ironed-red buzzing
       futures screaming

the black sun rose
so we could grow
beyond the poem

beyond the H-word end zones
lingering above and below
our resting realm

worm blood

my forever maggot brain
oh George

I let the black sun rise
because I do not mind ageing
eclipsed by creases
bigger than skin

I have given up on trying to hide the bags under my eyes

for they have become the A1 Dimo's—
the needed valleys in which cool grows
the speckled bed of shade where lightyears come to sleep

I let the black sun rise
because I am the beginning of fury

I have turned my ribs Eva
into the branched pace of Hesse trees
in order to bring my heart closer to sky

before you got here the air was brown
throat rough with frays of eruption
sternum forged from early stampedes / wind hooves
blood spit vestigials
rot prayers


I have let my toes become turbines to desert air
left my nails to be buried in mistakes of perfection

I let the black sun rise
    Yusef

because I am that black Komunyakaa
sun rose

older than when was
was was

I am not afraid to be great
without you

because after you
waaaaaay   after you

I'm still gonna be here

growing palms out the soul
of your Timbs

and all you gonna hear from the potion is

...next

## Branch Kids

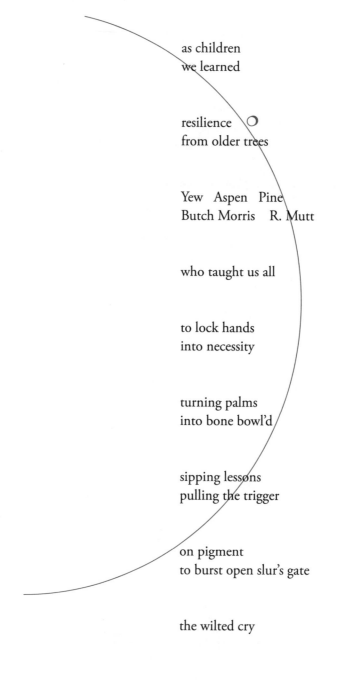

as children
we learned

resilience
from older trees

Yew   Aspen   Pine
Butch Morris   R. Mutt

who taught us all

to lock hands
into necessity

turning palms
into bone bowl'd

sipping lessons
pulling the trigger

on pigment
to burst open slur's gate

the wilted cry

leaving only stares
after the black fire


for us to climb
to "higher goals"

# Shooting Cee-Lo With Stephen Mallarmé

C'mon nigga
Don't miss your chance


You throw a 6 6 6
I'll buy the devil a twix


You throw a 4 5 6
I'll buy ya daddy 6 mo'



We can talk about symbolism on our way to the bank

## Sweet Agua-liita

in the same way the sun
has learned to hammer
hours of light
to the sky

drip back wet
to glimmering blur

we too    horizon
to say thank you

to ask you
sweet agua-liita

how are you?        O
has anyone asked?

do you need a break
from your slow serrating
sawing

back answers
into the earth?

tiding—
are you tired of her palms holding you?

are your own palms tired of being pitchers?

all the echoes
you've been pleating into the mountains

scribbles
      you've been scribbing into the sand

        extra broader
          than Broadway
            sizer than sizeway


sweet agua-liita we've come with basket ears
to gather your pours of wisdom

learn how to listen
  and crawl
      out from this durable darkness
            city
            escape into thick  rurals  of real night

              teach our hold the hand of empathy

                learn from the mirror in you
                and ask

              are we ok?

           what can we do?

            can you hear the fragrant *thank yous*
          from Aroma's soldiers wandering
        from lilies to lilacs

      every scent an homage
can you smell the hyacinths in the hallway?


we've asked wild's eyes to close

  so if you need to undress

and let your water water
  you can do so in a finally privacy
    tie your tears up for drying

      draping beauty

        is it ok if we weep with you?

          it's ok if you don't remember how to…

  waiting
  willowed over memories
              hunched
              into summer-heavy trees
                    leaning




                      into truth
                        off the end

                          of confessional limbs

                        juice
                        I love you



          have your waves aged with stretch marks?

        are your ripples not actually flexible?

      do you sometimes want to be prey?

      are these human metaphors unfair?

do you consider ice a cousin or an outfit?


but more than these questions

we've come here today

to say thank you

and to listen

to anything you have to say

and if that say is an ask for us to be quiet

then consider the rest of the poem unending

a silent party
praise

# Self Portrait

*for Pop Duke*

quiet as the Leica's metal lashes
blinking in the bed of my palm

this M4-2 has turned me into teeth
left me gnawing on New York

gnawing on barb wires in Brooklyn that crown
old fences— leaving Cy Twomblylylylylylylylyly
shadows laid up on 4pm sidewalks
real nigga shit

gnawing on the  UhOhh  in Mosholu Parkway
impatient laced arms and eyes cross arrowed
in a windowsill waiting
the image is in tension
the anatomy of framing

I gnaw on the East River as ripples curl
into the stiches of a thrown Baseball
while tugboats wish up chubby shores

I focus and gnaw lit pauses into the body
after the shutter Trinities with click

I take off my hat
and gnaw close at f-stop 2.8
and step into the mirror'd
depth of feeling

◯

# Haiku for both Bleecker Streets but...

the Bushwick version
is like a bacon-and-egg
with no roll or cheese

ooouuu

# For the Disappearance of our Neighborhoods

*Shout out R.T.C. yurrr*
*Shout out Baselitz*

in this version of the matrix—
we're eager at youth's pension

so we hang our retired
Nikes    black over the arpeggio

wet power-lines
braided block eyebrows

keeping the secrets
of a generations drip safe

in the sweet souls we hide
above street sweeping

where city kids know the difference
between nature and natural

SHAED and DINGE
sticking their bubble-gum tags

onto teethy walls
before the eventual chew

even if they swallow us whole
we still gonna be the shit
smeared. unforgettable. eternal.

# Diary From the Nigga in my Dreams

I want a carpet of clouds and a horizon-made mirror
and alongside the landscape of my entertained windows
I want emotional views of New York's bridges at sunset

I want a kitchen that smells like Flushing at all times
and comforters made of patchwork farm land
with boots of muddy puddles

I want scarfs made of long-winding rivers
and hand-made straw hats of hawk nests

I want fresh cigarettes made of charcoaled chimneys
and matches made of volcanos

I want gloves of summer's sand
and subway tunnel pockets
with the old Number 6 train for veins
its peeling red painted cars as blood


I want cotton for nothing but memories
and sugar cane just the same


but I do want a coat of the finest canopies
with a collar made of clay

and I do want notebooks
with silk pages
with lightning-bug filaments

and I want drawers of harvested winds
trousers of sea breezes

I want to eat only the richest dirt
and bathe in vats of mud

I want the soap of Shakespeare's bones
and the shampoo of Medusa's spit

I want pillows made of fresh snow
and sheets made of massages

I want the discipline of Adrian Piper
the sound of Bad Brains
the heart of Sonia Sanchez
I want to move like James Brown
be fearless like Michelle Obama
but I also want to become the darkness of Caravaggio

and I want desire

like the hidden half of D'angelo
when he asked the world

how does it feel ?

I want a mustache made of tall grass
simply to look like the portraits of my past

and I want a mouth made of lakes
with lips like waves

and I want to make love to a woman who's 1,000 feet tall
she'll laugh
and tell me I'm short
I'll laugh and tell her she's right

though big or little or brief
I'd barrow the brightness of a moon's full glow
turning moonshine to sugar cubes

and sweeten her tea

and when day fades
and her eyes become heavy with sleep
I'll blow out the flickering sun
turning night into moodshine

and laying with my dream-tress
I'd cup the night's sky

"I'm tired" she'd say— so I'd grab the stars
and hide them in my mouth
making every nigga in the south with fronts
pine over my new cosmic grill

there'd be nothing left
but the sounds of saint Trane
and a Gathering of Tribes

## While I take a bath, Ruth Asawa helps me think about loneliness, the flu and white supremacy

a fever
forces dark podiums
under my microphone eyes as I sink
into the heat water hush
to hush away

I swirl
bath waves into
siphons to drown hoof-hooded ripples
that gallop my body
of warmth

big Prince
of flood please
hurry and steal me from this fever so
melanin can swirl magic back
into me

I am
too beautiful and have too
much to do to let a slipping grip grab hold
of me or get in anyone's way
anymore

O

# On My Leo Shit

*cancer moon tho*

on trickling heels
of winter's thaw

I battle womb-given gifts
one messiah complex lie at a time

each tale
brings the heart's bend

closer to private break

the vessel-red bricks

blacken
with age

the body is still
fenced in

and the willow too
me afraid weeps

in deep
ego-shade

Dear July:
These "I promises"

are getting old—
so please peel back this prickled armor

and me let be
vulnerable too

# The No Scent Story

Once upon a time – I was backpacking in the Sierras with my friend's dog – Anais – we had been on the trail for a few days – hiking east – when we reached this bucolic valley bullied with tall blonde grasses swaying sweetly in this gentle and effervescent way – wind rushing its fingers thru the soft hair of the mountains – no one was around – and Anais was off chasing a squirrel or something else delicious and I found myself laying with one hand in this gushing stream – pushing itself slowly over the moss-softened rocks – gewy'd with green age – I melt-ly unbuttoned my pants – unbuttoning my guard as I loosened myself into the moment – my breath filled and deepened until it reached a new pace and my body hardened until I became the nature around me – flowering – sweet so soft – so wet I exhaled smiles out my flirt-so-wet eyes and at that exact moment – a man dressed in full military fatigues including a face mask and a hat worn eye low – holding a shotgun across his chest coughed to clear his throat aggressively – in the same breath that I reached this sloppy nirvana – I was stripped entirely of bliss and my sense of freedom abandoned me – I was drilled shit with fear – as this man stepped closer – I tried to pull up my pants despite still laying down – "son" he said – "you're sitting by my no scent" (a tool used by hunters) – I thought I misheard him – I tried to speak but could only mumble squeaks with the same syllables as words – "my no scent son" he pointed to an aerosol can – which was so unbelievably laying right next to me – "*no scent*" the can read "NO SCENT USES ENZYMES TO ENCAPSULATE AND <u>DESTROY</u> HUMAN SCENT" – what the fuck! as I threw the can in his general direction with my pants still handcuffed around my ass)  as he walked towards the can he ushered his deep and erect voice out his hidden mouth "you out here all alone? ... we're an awfully long way from the road" pumping and discharging his gun as he walked towards me – shells summersaulting like red flares whistling above a young boy's cry for help – "na fam – I got mad hittas up the trail – we're having a frat party here later –  like a really big frat party with really big frat dudes – and all my people is literally on the way" (when I get really scared I use the word *literally* and talk like I'm from the valley – I don't know why – it's a terrible defense mechanism – like fainting goats – or trumpets who're afraid of the band) I lied thinking about what kind of wreckable terror could ensue – he stood quietly for a moment – still like a radio tower soldering in the middle of empty field – he was expressionless – reaching for something in the air not yet attainable – after a moment – he backed up – put his gun over his shoulder – "you boys don't party too hard now ya hear" – Anais showed up late with a skull or hoof of some kind trying to impress me with her own hunting skills – her tail was wagging with pride and I stood up – laughing and crying hysterically – I shot-gunned a beer for reclamation and decided it was time to go home –

# In the Hold of an Uncertain Self

In this
   amulet life                    known pivot
      memorable                      tender rotation


                        where quietness —
                              narrates        my heart
                              tension         tends to tear


         tho fleeting currents wash our weak


                  I am


         splitting against the undertow


on one end                                          and the other
order                          O                     luck
discipline                                           chaos
curfew                                               pleasure



                  I am


      genuinely shook
       to be drawn
      too far to either side
        for a great fear



            I'll never make it
               bac

k

to
the
mid
dle
                    or the other side
                              ever again

*Did you shoot em*

*Na kid I didn't have the balls*

*That's when I realized im bumpin too much Biggie Smalls*

— Fugees

# Both Sides of the Cover: Part I

untied by the open exposure of evening's blur
I emptied my Frankenthaler shadow
into bed with a lit Camel and a new spectrum of violence
that climbed in from the open window


at first words were slapped back and forth
but quickly turned into the sad sound of fists
scraping concrete and faces and some rough
minutes later my neighbors from across


the hall joined in the ooouuuing with their own
dry opera of bed springs booing in-sync rhythms
mirroring the motion of gloves doubling up
above the sweat-stained grey ring


the noise funneling into my bedroom
Morpheus'd under the scorched sky
while me and my Helenus shadow sat up listening
to the twin-sounds pour down from open-mouth clouds

                    I remember

being everything but envious of both situations
while I tried to come up with a poem:

## Both Sides of the Cover: Part II: The Poem

my shadows favorite
character is the oracle

draped in acrylic-
washed linen

bending over the dark
of evenings blur

to blow out
fidgeting light

until Camels get tamped
into stained glass stadiums

      old crumpled smiles
          burnt yellow

◯        ash scatter hooves
         pre-owed bodies
       muted in the wreck

    left beside rouge embers
growing old

their grey whispers kissing
any glimpse of daylight

left from the window
while two twin sounds
pour'd down from open mouths

they came—

at the same time

exhaling yesss's

but after the encore
all that remained

was poetry's violence
of omission

## Nature Walk

*For Camille T. Dungy and her Black Nature anthology*


Some people stay up at night wondering what stars are made of
While other people sleep great knowing that most stars we can see
have already died


I've never slept


as time is an alarm
waking us up to the realization
that earth has already shattered
and the shatter spins faster
than light as we know it


But these days
While the light is good
I walk around New York

And see other people as if they were trees
In the woods

Each one unique and perfectly beautiful
But if I stop and wonder about each one

I'll never get where I'm going
Or see the forest-treat in front
Of my eyes

# Elegy

the way that white
crooked Lubriderm
spout piddles squish

into the weak
fabric of your
mug-shot palm

hurts the same way I hate
you think lotion does
the same thing as lube

the memory of that
bottle is raw
the way your wet

hair used to whip
off your sweat and land
on my back like lashes

I can tell by the way
your body quivers
when I call you daddy

that you've been
lied to your entire life
I imagine that's why

you've ended
up with me
but when I left


you that day I couldn't
hold in a fart and I wondered
if you've ever been embarrassed

## Staring Into the Spitten Image

washed up on the bruised intersection
of Broome and Bowery's splintered cross

lay the driftwood of a man
full robbed of roots

O

(who looked just like me)

all branch
gum-flat on the curb

I stood watching
his body

a holed boat's need
for land

O

his eyes
gone year'd
with sea crumbs and wrong turns

he held a vanity mirror
saying goodbye
to each of the 37 million bacteria
that would be leaving his face that day

one by one he thanked them all for coming
fluttering lashes each prettier than the last

thank you thank you

ohhhhh   it is   so   gooood   to   see
me

isn't it?

(he laughed like Lana Turner finally taking O'Hara's advice)

— thank you

he stood up
and swung
himself into traffic
like untied bags of free'd secrets
buoying
bobbing
completely unafraid

as if he knew
earth had already shattered years ago
but came back in time
to tell the rest of us to

—*takecare*

when I looked back
he was gone

○

and a young kid
with arms T'd on his hips
looked up at me and said

"Hey Mista—

Aint you afraid of getting hit by them cars?"

I felt new waves crashing over me

his mother snatched his hand and yelled

"get away from that shipwreck boy!"

# When An Angel Gets Wings

*Scene: The Popeyes on Atlantic and Ralph Ave (true story)*

after death brought to me its flowers—
leaked pain through a brittle procession of smiles
I returned to the wilted rifle that stole

me from the crumb-rubble
delicious chicken and once again
marinated in that film of thigh'd air

and now with wings of my own I fluttered
above        with crystalline vision        a conversation
between three elders discussing the well-

being of their youngest grandson
whose only wish was for a pair
of brand new Air Jordans

    Now shit goddam— is it fair for us to pay

    The route of someone else? Or should we carve

    Into the record a new groove where he can then

    Wholly understand that outliers always win in the long run?

    If you give a young nigga a lil' bit information now

    What you paying for is way more than now can ever know

    Shit! Er'body know that

the air dappled my wings
like conk settin' in
as I settled over their wisdom

listening to their echo slap the linoleum
checkered floor with sage grace
of how to raise a child with love

but at that moment the poem broke
and a text message came through
to one of the elder's phones

any yall niggas know how to spell

E – U – R – O – P – E

one elder asked the others

they then tagged together
every unthoughtof combination
of letters imaginable

sometimes starting why    y
and ending with    u

they tried to remember
stolen lessons from
the Gullah horizon

but it was then in the shotgun of insult
where a white team of snickering kids

sat at a nearby table
laughing with loaded pain

they shot
and I was hit in the ricochet
died on impact

because even under the armor of brilliance
sometimes the weight of shame

stings a hole so sho nuff
there's nowhere to hide

and to the sum of kids who trot
on the high backs of "education"

thinking wisdom lives
in the arrangement of European letters

jousting unfairly
into the hearts of the other-wised

I say you
how could you

I say you
goddam

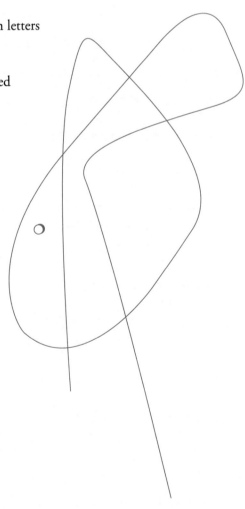

## Love Haiku for You When Things Feel Difficult But It's Ok for Things To Be Difficult Because Things Aren't Always in a Rigid Binary and Sometimes Things Can Be Nasty but Also Be Sweet and Ok Too Like Pickling

I love you more than
Cabbage loves sealed tight jam jars
With big time to rot

## Missed Photograph

inside an iron balcony above the streets of Williamsburg
a small group of Hasidic children point and laugh playfully
at another group of children across the street


on the lower half of the frame— a dark-skin man stands
on a sky-lift fixing wires of a telephone pole


the objective of the image:

the kids aren't pointing at this man
but the assumption is that class and race
are illuminated by height
and the luxury of laughter

## Thit Life

*A special moment for all the real hoes*

don't ever call anyone
you love

a hoe

and mean it
in a bad way

or in any way
that doesn't mean

I love you so much
and I love how brave

and fun and smart you are
so don't call anyone

a     T.H.O.T.

before calling yourself
    a     T.H.I.T    "that hoe <u>IN THERE</u>"

and have the "in there"
be your heart and the way

you relate to your confident
and proud selves

so younger people
who are beginning

to think about

sexuality and other

cool stuff too can see
there's no shame

in being
who we are!

Rip this page out and fold it so it fits in your wallet
When the time is right — give it to someone special

# Controversial and Erotic Dreams Where the New World Trade Center is the Largest Klansman in the United States and As it Turns Out We're Engaged

in platform Camo Crocks
and a tommy girl sweater
I feel cute and can see
my eyes asking and answering
the same question with
eyelashes batting longer
than ocotillos in full desert bloom
I'm walking down the aisle
looking up at my groom
who's veiled in applause
girdled in trust I don't recognize
but no one's ever doubted my slut life
consistencies *THITTY-LIFE* on god
so I pull up that pretty hood slow
lifting the great weight of American linen
off the burdened shoulders of a sequel

to see the real face of world trade hiding
behind two rigid eyes carved out of steel
keeping an erect gaze on us all
my groom starts to shimmy up its white
robe sinking to its knees kissing me
until my back Wall Streets with joy
but just then my panoptic mascot
starts to cough and deteriorate
each I-beam vertebrate gagged
ripped from its escalator neck
every window throated with bigotry
crashes onto the sidewalk like tear bombs
I cum to the realization that
my fiancé has exploded

I stand in front of the rubble terrified
while a new flag of freedom is waving
from out the detritus— I wake up
thinking about love and pareidolia
and the new-old hood worn
on the new world trade

# The Mascot of my KKKontroversial dreams

# On the Count of 3:

1. there are no clocks in prison ( full stop )
   for people doing time

   only repeat chain booms
   breaking the sound of closeness

2. I ask a young man on Rikers Island
   why he doesn't want to go "home"

   and he tells me
   nigga  I am  "home"

2. is the way Jim Crows and Crows

2. is the other day— I saw a husky lose a fight
   to a cat and I cried— not because I felt bad
   for the dog but because I know the motor
   of slavery is fear

2. is the way bleached Jesus looks and acts like a pencil eraser

2¼. its hard enough to convince white America that Black
   Lives have always been of Matter

2½. we will not be etcetera to someone else's doom-sex fetish
   (Derek Chauvin)

2¾. it's time you knew that

3.

## Untying Dream Knots
## and Chewing on Badge Juice


I take the Blue Pill

and hide inside the lyrics of a wound

O      standing behind the waiting side of a podium

                barreled
                in a hall full of cops

                who stand in a semicircle
        behind the Merovingian

        like seeds to a halved melon

        on the other side
of the precinct

is our people

the other half
    the melonated half

            oxidized
            browned
                    beautiful

        their rebounding ears
            in the air
            as I speak

                police precincts need to blossom
                into epicenters of art movements

no longer petal on pain like flowers
who don't give a bloom about us

the Merovingian and his pupils
boo'd from behind their badges

I keep going

if there's going to be any change
in the way the color blue whines

we need violence against the knees on our necks
and bigger matches for better fires

but we also need comradely in the heart of the precinct

we need to incentivize our police to encourage themselves

we need pay raises for every non-violent month

added vacation time for adding patience into the potion

new horses for every time we don't need to call hearses

gold stars for every gold cap that isn't fired

we need to be melting unused bullets into real gold caps
for crooked teeth and have a contest to see which cop can
smile and imitate the cosmos most best

we need to turn the locker room talk out
with the same clout that cuddles
up to the shoulders of autonomy

but we also need posters of Muhammed Ali in holding cells

and texts by Rumi and Phillis Wheatley on the walls

so we can see honor the same way we see capes and cake

and we need to be listening to tree and dirt histories so we
        too can grow
with wisdom and leafed up / mushroom excellence


◯


    I take the Red Pill

and can no longer hide inside the wound

so I crawl out from under the chorus
of gunshots

    where different blue and red
      lights heave

    in flung wide figure 8's—

and the police fly on their sirens
from wing to wing—

like speed skaters shifting
their weight from leg to leg

one of them turns up the static on their walky talky radio
to drown the glittering now pouring pain
out the hole in the neighborhood

*did you see what happened?* —Fred Hampton

buried away
in the single blink a secret needs to hide

a nightstick

is limping
into the damp end
of a bleached christening

*who was it? —George Floyd*

a cold—
the sick color of teething beasts

*was anyone home? —Breonna Taylor*

eyes falling
into fractures of denial

*What else did you hear?*

*−I heard−*

they left the open mouth
of their radios running
so puddles of static
would drown out the hummed lyrics
of tragedy tunes

# *−I hearrrd−*

they rolled the shimmer of broken silver
on the ground like cobalt demons
sprinkling dice in their hands

so they could blame the peopled odds on chance

they let the blue static spill over the crescent children

whose mouths were at the beginning of their smiles

*−I heard−*

                              the static had sounded like hearses
                              pummeling over pebbles in the yard
                                            as it rolled up to the mortuary


*— I   heard —*

                    all that was left
                    was static

              like the worst advice telling a community to

        ssSssHHHHHhhhhhhh



                                          O

                              beside the wound

                              I called the nearest precinct of trees
                              to tell them I found their birds

                              but all I got was Agent Smith
                              whispering like static

                              and the sound of vultures
                              pecking at melonated fruit

                              I turned on the light
                              and hung up the phone

                              ignored the glitching cat



Outside the phone booth I saw N.H. Pritchard
holding a sign that read    "I hate to say I told you so"

## The Origins of White Guilt

cotton clings sheepishly
to embarrassed branches
thrashing with whispered apologies

each knuckle-hung finger woven
into the nappy kaleidoscope
has heard the bitter sweet blip
                    *imsorry*—

hushed under loosened bails of
sprawling air like salt-fire flames crying
onto an oily coal for atonement

# El Lissitzky's Red Wedge

*for Chenee Daley*

Red wedge =
My niggas

And by writing nigga
I mean nigga
Not the agent
of appropriation
Not the scrolling tongue slip blurted by our tumblr-fed mouths

Not yet

Red wedge =
That that thin-thin that teeters
On either side of the that-that rotting gallow
Separating us from internet-misshaken identities
And all those swollen identities
But no thanks I'm an influenzer
And Harryette Mullen's-Root
Must be affecting our dream's cause
Last night I woke up in Red Wedge


Red wedge =
Either you're with me or offence me

In the suburbs
To a mother I had never seen before
Saying
Good morning my nigga
Have I ever told you
You look an awful lot like that one story
Brotha Malcolm and the big black wedge

Black Wedge =
Malcolm

Black Wedge =
Malcolm

Black Wedge =
Malcolm

Black Wedge =
Malcolm

Black Wedge =
Malcolm

Black Wedge =
Malcolm

Black Wedge =
Malcolm

Black Wedge =
Malcolm

Black Wedge =
Malcolm

And the splitter
And the maul
And the hawk
Who can always see
That when I put the black letters of my niggas
In between the emptiness of these white pages
You too read them as 'my niggas'
Say it as 'my niggas'
Divorced from the black wedge
And the wet mirror and you

And I don't know if that's regressive
Or socialist
But a teacher once told me about someone
Named Osip Mandelstam
And now that's my nigga too
And that makes things all the more confusing
But don't that just beat beat all


Beat the whites =
A language no less a commodity
Than poetry is for sale


Beat the whites =
When I say my niggas
I really really mean I love you

# Thoughts on Reparations / Teaching on Rikers Island / An Owed Rebate for This Beautiful Beautiful Wild

the COs on Rikers Island
think they work in Plato's Cave

the way they treat their own
shadows
like dirges

won
trophies

to be sung
over cells

but that so
is so not our song

nor has the key jangle snare
ever been the rhythm

the way we skate
into moons
apostrophized glow

menthol shush
every night

letting the whisper
brush

kinks
back

into
silence

O

littered wishbones
 get pushed into shoe-broomed corners
    for juju

because when we fight back
we do not use luck
we use ritual and disciple

and sing
to a very different
            hand-clapped
tempo

and when we dance
we pick up
pin-hole star-bright
residue

off the tops of clouds
and stretch them into conga's

beating a new sound
into the halls

like M'tume and Miles

kisses between air

and its melted binge
of a loosened-belt
horizon

Dear Damon T. Hininger:
"rehabilitation" does not look like the money in your wallet
and if you really think it does
then I really think you owe us all
quite a bit a lot of that money

**Interlude**

if you're ever walking around New York
keep your eyes peeled for thumb-sized
du-rags (with the cape flyin)
tied to gingko tree branches
I been putting my niggas on the map
so we always got soldiers on our side
(with the wood grain) the gap
tooth leaf plus the du-rag combo
look like Laurence Fishburne or Seal
when he got that Drip Check from
the Batman Soundtrack in the 90's
no cap

# An Ongoing Portion of Colored Numerals

*(sketches from the notebook)*

New numbers for every time I've been called black
And then leaned into what it means to define color or be defined by color

1.  **Gelatin Silver**
     carving a swan's contour out of silence
     I jump into the muted beak and blur of William Klein
          throat-locks unlock and I sing
               inside the softness of chrysalis kingdoms

73. **Tissue Red**
     a type of depression that patience would kill for

6.  **Soft Velvet Yellow**
     where I sit next to the rolled down window of summer
     watching pedestrian life spider by like streamers
     twinkling on new handle-bar'd air

6 ½. **Less Soft Velvet Yellow**
     winter comes back     again
     for its throne of pejorative shawls

     distant warmth of august— reflecting smiles
     off the murky cesuras

**221. Itchy Beige**

    where birds sing debris songs into new nests


**300. Futurely Umber**

    the inconscious reminder
    that's there is nothing rotten
    for the soul haunters to hunt for


**181. Dried Bird-of-Paradise Brown**

    A slowness so precious it's priceless

## A Plath and Blaxploitation

if I were a betting man
I'd drive up hwy 395

towards Nevada
make a left before death

valley to put money
down that Sylvia Plath

thinks the night sky
is God wearing black face

or a blaxploitation of
modern light

considering dawn
a sink to wash away

the minstrelsy
every morning

I'd win that bet
a great grip of pouty money

drink *nigger / berried* wine
to celebrate in shadows

oscillate wildly
wrestling with the pros

and cons
of cancel culture

## "Hysteria"

she came across
a knife in Bedstuy

while doing dishes
in her suddy sink

when a Gale                    pushed her
        Of                           into complete
        Darkness               distrust and fear

she fell into a sudden daydream
        red cloud fantasies
        pour'd mosaic scatter
            gasp down her arm

            blood flowers
        deprived of   (fresh)   air
    flew out the nightmare

                    O

when she woke up
her eyes came back the kitchen
    sickened

by how closely the thought must have lived

there was no sign

    of death blooming around
        she cried

    but no one
was home

## Ember

when it was time for bed

we would beg

my mother

for the closeness

we needed

in the same way

the cherried ember

to her cigarettes

would always beg

my mother

for one more breath

we would wait

her cigarettes and I for

pleading for love

in the same way

I would have died

to have been the only

glowing pulse

she needed

it always felt so

sad to have to compete

with a box of Marlboro lights

# The Vineyard
*Black Daphne*

○

our sister's darker psalms were abandoned behind the barn on the old
family vineyard— my brothers and I watched her from the other side of
the closed kitchen window day after day as she tried to crawl back from
the slit in the barbed wire fence she was trying to escape in the thick
         air of her own handed elegies

○

she cried— mimicking the licking movements of winds tongue slap
with each mopping step her ploughed pose slowered her into a warm freeze
became her body's dialect and dirt grove her heels
         into a shackled still— she reached up

○

snapping branches above her braids so the natural adhesive sap
would slip down her skin stuck— the homeless foliage swirling
around her soon laid down its Fall sleeping pad and she
         embedded in the grounds of gods

○

blazed into winters forever cold arriving with burrs her knees
began to root by the un-plucked harvest of grapes her arms
became black 10,000 tannins her mouth ovaled age and out poured
         a plum-colored hum down her bark-peeling chin

○

my sister had always been told that the blacker the berry the sweeter the juice
but she hadn't realized that meant she would eventually become the vineyard
too and the pain of being alone while her brothers stood around watching
         from the other side of a closed window

## Short Poem of Gratitude For the Anomaly Intersections Around NYC Whose Often Overlooked Crosswalk Signs Are Permanently Fixed on the Walk Icon and Never Ever Show the Don't Walk Icon

You always are
The poem I am trying to write

Your encouragement
Goes a long way

Thank you

# Thumb Songs

lined in palm-smear
      & ghost breath
         heat

me and Siever stood p o t i e n t l y

    in a toe-willing July

slow-braised in yuck
    with freaks

who all freak in physical verbatim
    under the M train

        where bodies ferment in K2 / kim-chi
        stained air by Kosciusko

            O

over Broadway the subway yawns
    while the shoe sound of Hip Hop walks with Bushwick

by Myrtle a man takes off his high hat and symbol
    when a sway with braids— car washed down the street

I tired to walk down Kossuth but fell face first into the braids
    slipping off the topple side of a teeter-heavy decision

sliding back into a time where muddied hands dug
    at the end of pivot queens

weaving maps with fingers harp ready
      bigger than spirit pluck


their hands swung like children using DNA strands to double dutch thru
    fields of wild hair— waving off contests of Evil


THIS POEM IS FOR THE WOMEN I SAW HIDING SEEDS
AND BRAIDING MAPS  INTO AND WITH EACH OTHER'S
HAIR DURING SLAVERY SO WHEN THEY WOULD RUN
AWAY FROM PLANTATIONS THEY WOULD ALWAYS HAVE
A REFERENCE FOR WHERE TO LOOK FOR FREEDOM
AND BEAUTY

ALTERNATE TITLE...... PYSCHIC CARTOGRAPAHY


    I saw thumbed crossovers sing
      "we can and do need each other"

    once over the other
      the other of the other   O   tuft

    soft with praise
      mosaic with promise

I saw their hands myth
    into future thanks

    I saw women using their clairvoyance
      like flashlights
        for the no doubt
          and soon-already-come darkness


      it's the most amazing thing I've ever seen

# Nature Haiku with My Hittas

in our new canoe
we paddled thru the Bronx zoo
black as Flaneur night

(shout out Lee and Marco)
Yo tu sabes mi Bapi's
Dejen de pelear)

## City Horses

malleable horizon     fire

                           ○

                  the ivory
                  tusks             of the ivy league
HAVE BEEN CUT!
                        we cut
them
                        to
                  shut up
                      the
conduit

                                    in this p       ress
          above dust
                l   ight

                    we
wor  s h I p escape hatch
                  against
        infinite leave

                b   east  s should n ever
beg
             the     c I tadel
           to be
                                  hung

s  tair we  ll  l h o   se
        flat
          in gray
            folds
                collects age

un dern
eath flicke ring

w
a
i
t

the
florescent wish
is floor
by floor to be
fuller

when
city horses

e s ca p e

I promise
the feral
sense
of home

there
will be
no waiting

nece◯ssary

## Medication Don't Teach the Distractions
## How To or Why To Behave

for every lullaby stuck in a gap-toothed night
there's another demon-sized light wave

pulling custody over my darkness
with gun-sacred blows and cry powder

ripping my copper ego that was trying
to patina and I know I need this quiet

without hiding but all I know of silence
is a hunt for louder distractions

like kids cutting holes in the sky at bed time
to let in knocking noise of saw and harder stardust

Shout Out Matta-Clark
Who been way ahead
Ever since he cut the line

76

# The importance of telling "The Facts" to fuck off

*For Saint Taylor Sakarett*

Never before
Have I been less interested in "The Facts"


     The way they grow
Into bubbled numbers
Of I told you so

1. New York City was built on a landfill
2. The lighter was invented before the match
3. There are 5 million trillion trillion bacteria on earth
4. Which is the same number as 4 quadrillion quadrillion
5. Wheels were a good idea…
6. This
7. That

                  I'm over it

                Fuck
                "The Facts"


I'd rather be given a carriage and a handful of spokes
Than be given the wheel

The readymade wheel is too predictable

Always the same motion
Again    and again

Who wants to be reminded of the ouroboros?

The seam always eating itself

The seam always losing

Not us

We demand options that taste like movement
And makes us feel like mangos

Into and outoo of time
Unpeeled and strung with the perfect pulp for sucking
I love it when you suck and fuck in my teeth
The hair in the brush
Don't ever clean up this love

Keep the facts

We want the opposite of facts
"in – facts"
"un – facts"

    The un – in the impossible
      The un – in the upside-downable

And the fracture after the il-facts

    That allows mountains to cry like unbitten-into-cupcakes
      Sweeter than ripe sprinkles waiting for the first smiling bite
            To burst open the seal

    In-factual light
      Like windows learning to crawl after the rock's last shatter

We're learning
To weave
Our mouths

From myth
In order
To breathe
An air
That tastes
Like quiet
After haikus—

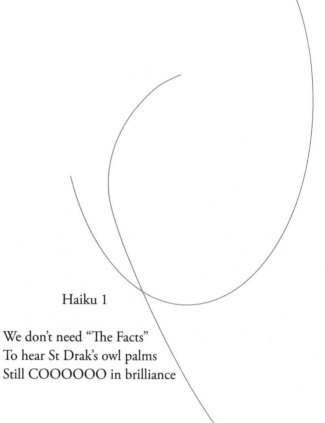

Haiku 1

We don't need "The Facts"
To hear St Drak's owl palms
Still COOOOOO in brilliance

We need you to know
That the sound of the 7 train
Is in-factually made of maple
And cedar pheromones
Pulsing

And if you listen close enough

You can still hear the engine reminisce

"we can
and and do
need – ee – eed
e – e – ch – other"

and the train rolls back
to pivot queens weaving maps

And
Hidden
In the slow ember
Of the way Taylor says

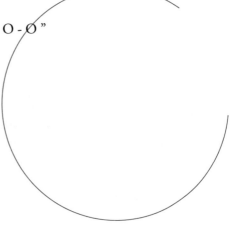

" ...Y - O - O - O - O - Ø "

Is a slanted smile
And tongue
So tough
And warm

Its learned to lick
The rough edges
Of ripped light
In order to soften
The rays
For the rest of us
To rest upon
Forever

"The Facts"

Know nothing
About what it means

To dance or smell like shit
In a basement with no money
But your best friends
And the ecstasy comes from the comfort and joy of being
Close to your people but the feeling of ecstasy also comes from the
    ecstasy we took

The way Taylor taught us to scream
With our names in our teeth
So perfect for shredding pain
Off our hearts

Taylor
    You taught us to never wipe away the mud
                            Or hide the mess from our families

                        We are who we are

O              So we let the dirt dangle over
                    To show the world
                    How siq our shit really is

            Fuck "The Facts"
        And the way reason has wronged us

        You'll always be here more than proof
    Because facts don't teach us about truth
    Or what it means to belong and love and why

# Mo' Dirt For Henry Threadgill During Quarantine

Between daylight's thinning blue appeal
    And the eventual press of night's flamboyant stare

Uncle Henry sat up in the crib wishing the wood floor
    Would just hurry up and cover itself in pre-echelon dirt

So he could join the ignint worms busied blind by instinct
    Swim in varicose castles chewed millennia

He wanted his skin cradled in minerals of rock queens
    Pounded pounded

Bored open mouths— viola sounds
    Filled with the blood engine of tongues

    O

Doing his air addition the homebound conductor crossed
    His plus signs with both hands behind the couch

Making wing-aged signals sing back
    Into the empty chamber

He wished for dirt and mo' dirt when his windows got too raw
    And he could no longer hide from the view looking back in at him

# When You're Hot for the Blues

when you're hot for the blues
there's no new nothing you can do

no new breaths
no new sound
no new poems

no leftover sight for eye lashes
to nibble on later

no new pain for the body
to call the future for

there's no new nothing you can do

except think of her
and how that too
aint really no new

especially when y'all aint got no honest right
being together in the first place      anyway

and all she want to do is wiggle
and be sweet      with you

and do that thing
she know how to do
so terribly terribly well

make you want to scream
and break all your Lightning Hopkins records

then find yourself tryna glue them broken records

back together again at 2:00 AM
cause your partner won't listen
and left you for rotten

but that sweetie pie slice
of secret ice cream cake you've got
is still whispering from the top of the dessert menu
talking about

what's it gonna be   daddy?

# Nightly Ouroboros

it's usually when the last light is turned off
when you decide it's time to tiptoe into my empty

brown cowboy boots and corral a whole heaven
of undealt evil onto the exact spot where I was gonna try

and get some sleep but now I'm up wondering why
you're never free for a 2:00 PM whistle with a glass of water?

how you're more like a lost colony
trying to beg its way back onto the map with apologies

or like a runaway cross trying to pray its way back
into the church but either way you're less

like magic every time you show up trying new tricks
to keep me from dreaming cause it's dawn now and I can see

you ain't nothing more than me
and that silent fang that slithers in with old guilt

biting just enough to be reminded that you love
being a pebble on the wrong side of the soul

## "Sweet-boy your eyes" // "Keep Going"

you don't have to anymore—

sweet-boy your eyes
into the wet worship machine

the way it leaves you every time
hungover the mania spout

making promises
with wilt and air

drained buzz
pinkened beds

○

you don't have to sweet-boy
your eyes

for all that glittery dust
prickle

there's still room to be anything
Black

sweet-boy your eyes away
from death that isn't yours

sweet boy your eyes

your eyes can still be
your eyes

## Dear DMX

*4.11.21*

yesterday

sitting on the J train
tears wheelied out my eyes

when the Ruff Ryders' anthem covered
the whole car with that bone-bristled intro

that perfect rhythm had the conductor yelling
*I'm bout to lose my mind— up in here*

*up in here—*    we nodded rockin'
together slow-sweet with shrugged faces

like the smell of your sound was too raw

but as the windows drove over the east river
we watched the clouds split so the sun could freely " whuuuut ! "
        with you

the way so many of us
want to say thank you

for saying what we didn't know how to say
or have the strength to understand way back in the day

## Love Poem

when I hear those whispers moon
out your crescent mouth

dressed in criminally
innocent smiles

cracked open
so culprit laugher

like crooked stars snapping their points off
for the pawn shop re-up

I re-so fall
in love
with you
again
everyday


melt beside your free-so tongues
so side-effect wild


abandoned train track
grass gorgeous

dry aqueduct perfect

the way metal has learned to rust
in order to make it back to nature

I wonder too if you can see me rusting
tryna make it home to the nature in you

*talk-to-me-nice*   ◯   *you say*

  under suck-tooth missives
              shucked from night-shells

              so under the beak
              I'm learning

      *es lo mismo so que—*

  wince pleasure
    sweetest pain
  first sips from fridge-cold mezcal


*pero la vina es so simplemente major*
or so I've heard

  when we met    ◯

    I brought flowers I picked from in between the city's missings

    lilies and wild tulips with haikus
      cute shit

        written about the way I wanted to so and so
          sweet with you
          and you

            cause I thought I was a bad nigga
            and I wanted you to too

                but you brought a bouquet of stolen thunder
                    from some hush-now-babied lightning storm

              cause only you
                the most oouu'est baddy

*te so amo-sote*

know how to talk a cloud
into giving away

## Sweet Flypaper

there are still birds
whose song outsweets
the thieving beaks
of nectar beggars

and there are still brown people
in Harlem

still smiles that smile so smile
still laughs that laugh so laugh

and there are still brown people
in Harlem

## To my niece Sweet Layla New Hip Hop Martei

when you decided so sweet
it was time to be

I was swimming in the ocean
unbuckled wet

under moonlight
waiting for your signal

to light up the night
grain sky          ◯

and so you did— and so did I—
dry off and drive up the spirit line

straight from Miami
with sorcery-ish-ness

to make it to your mother's New York coronation
she was glowing so beautiful

to welcome her baby queen back
from the well-fitting gowns of heaven

I wouldn't have missed it
for all the get out of hell free cards

or dope-full pockets of liable prayers
to see your father standing there

riveted perfect proud squeaking
into earned silence

your grandparents crying
with creased smiles

forever unfolding still
my sweet new Layla New Hip Hop Martei

you joined our Nature that day my Nigga and I love you
no matter what side of the wish

bone breaks in your little palm
lined with potience

and thank you

for teaching us
a new 5 letter word

for joy


—your uncle Basie


holla at me when you ready to go fishing
I've got two poles and good maps that need using

and a permanent seat for you in the canoe
no backsies !

# For the Disappearance of our Neighborhoods
*Alt Take*


in this version of the Matrix—
we're eager at youth's pension

so we hang our retired

Nikes   over powerlines
that jellyfish black

over the city's hood
like visible tendons
to invisible prettier wings

swooping under the NYC
maintenance suit blue sky

where our shoes hang like cyphers and freestyles
spit verses and finger quotes
quoting air's emptiness

we throw our shoes up
on powerlines
so myth clings to pulse

like a ventriloquist with a wand
when you see our FILA's

you will mutter the same syllables
as Mi Lady's bar and grill on Prince
where I once wore a crown

your mouth will mutter out the sound of shadows
from under the trophies of your tongue's uneven memory

mutter the same syllables of laughter
that used to pour out the back of your favorite bar
like wet operas spilling again and again until the sips are all gone

we throw our shows up
on powerlines

so electricity can drip into laughter
because we all know
how a smile can iron in some sweet
where it don't belong

we throw our shoes up
on powerlines

so our laces
can live like hair leftovers

falling from the million arms
of our grandmothers' favorite brushes

the brush holds back and whispers
go on sweet baby
mama's got you

we throw our shoes up
on powerlines

like bubble gum
sticking-in big city braces

I am not ashamed of inconvenience
and I promise to ruin everything

even though Kamau told us
"it is not enough"

I will try
to slow up the monster
I will try
before it incinerates us all

I will turn this poem
into a sword
and slip it in the NYT's real estate section
and if anyone sees a condo for sale on Avenue D
and doesn't think about the consequences
the poem will know to stab their thumbs
just enough so they hear
someone else's hands covering they face
when the sheriff shows up
holding a piece of paper
that weighs more than the contents of the whole block

we throw our shoes up
on powerlines
above the intersections we've come to know as home


and say what up when you see me
I'll dap you up and call you god

we can rest by the SEN4 hydrants
smile in the SHAED
smile In the DINGE


we throw our shoes up
on power lines
because

it's something like rearranging the ABC's
so it starts with the LES's
and end with my niggas

**Shoutout**
**all the carousel operators who helped me around the way**

Kevin Broderick. Erik Jacobson. Alan Gilbert. Aunty and Uncle Ashe. Parisha Pakroo. Patricia Silva. Derek Walcott. That Biggie Smalls Cassette. Adrian and Chan. Gaby, Julia Gulia, and Smevs. La Wood Familia: Sievey, Pete, Killa, Al. My Silver Towers Clique. Ali T. Goya Maceira. Cara Marie Carla. Quik Trak. Dixie and Spike. Big Papo and MUD home for wayward boys. Benny and Maxy Baby. Triangle Heart. Taylor Sakarett. RTC and the 4WD's. Walker—whose always got me covered. Emil. Jota y David. Fat Tony y Jeneva. Joe Riley and Audrey Snyder. My 93 4Runna Gunna. Mihn's Auto Repair Shop in San Diego. Yaya, Cojo, and Layla Hip Hop. My Oakland family. My ATL Family. The Greater Allen Foundation and Casandra Sweet So Mayela.

Earlier versions of some of these poems were first published in *American Chordata*, *Beacon Quarterly*, *Black Renaissance*, *Recliner Mag*, and *Post Road Magazine*.

Special shoutout to Chico Herbison
A bad nigga— whose mentorship is invaluable
Thank you


Extra big up:
Matvei Yankelevich
Daniel Owen

And the UDP fam


   To all y'all
My most best thank yous is due